T0065117

The NO WORRIES WORKBOOK

124
- ✔ LISTS,
- ✔ ACTIVITIES, &
- ✔ PROMPTS

to GET OUT of YOUR HEAD
— and ON with YOUR LIFE!

MOLLY BURFORD

ADAMS MEDIA
NEW YORK LONDON TORONTO SYDNEY NEW DELHI

This book is dedicated to my mother, Amy.
Her relentless kindness and her ability to prevail even
in the most trying times never ceases to amaze me.

adamsmedia

Adams Media
An Imprint of Simon & Schuster, Inc.
100 Technology Center Drive
Stoughton, MA 02072

First Adams Media trade paperback
edition November 2019

For information about special
discounts for bulk purchases, please
contact Simon & Schuster Special
Sales at 1-866-506-1949 or
business@simonandschuster.com.

The Simon & Schuster Speakers Bureau
can bring authors to your live event. For
more information or to book an event
contact the Simon & Schuster Speakers
Bureau at 1-866-248-3049 or visit our
website at www.simonspeakers.com.

Interior design, hand lettering, and
images by Priscilla Yuen

Manufactured in the United States
of America

6 2022

Library of Congress Cataloging-in-
Publication Data has been applied for.

ISBN 978-1-5072-1156-4

CONTENTS

INTRODUCTION 7

HOW TO USE THIS BOOK 9

ACTIVITIES 11

Break Up with Worry! 12

Explore Meditation 13

Rearrange Your Room 14

Make an Anti-Worry Playlist . 16

Give Yourself a Hand 17

Stop the Spiral! Try One of
These Ten Things to
Do Instead 18

Color Your Way to Calm:
Mandala 20

Sip Some Tea 21

Find Your "It's Okay"
Reminders 22

Track Your Location 24

Take Your Ticket for a
Worry-Free Day 25

Get It in Writing! 26

Kick FOMO to the Curb 28

Embrace Uncertainty 29

Face Worst-Case Scenarios
Head-On 30

Water Your Growth 32

Spin This Decision Wheel 33

Make a Plan 34

Peer Into This Crystal Ball 36

Appreciate These Ten
Beautiful Little Things 37

Look Ahead 38

Complete a Self-Care
Checklist 40

Connect the Dots................. 41

Wake Up with a Mantra 42

Take Belly Breaths................ 44

Draw Your Worries 45

Reroute the Train Wreck of
Thought 46

Look at What's Going *Right* .. 48

Draw Your Jealousy 49

Discover How Worry Is in
Your Way 50

Pop a Balloon! 52

Draw Your Happiness 53

Scribble Your Way to Sleep .. 54

Color Your Way to Calm:
Koi Pond 56

Do the Animal ABCs! 57

Take a Smaller Step! 58
Explore the Pros and Cons .. 60
Unplug! 61
Discover Your Purpose 62
Relax with Guided Meditation
   1: Breathe In Calm;
   Exhale Hope 64
Send a Text 65
Map Out Your Future Self 66
Take a "Walk" 68
Write a Letter to Future You ... 69
Rewrite the Story You Tell
   Yourself 70
Give Thanks 72
Ride the Wave 73
Rediscover the Real You 74
Cross Out Your Mistakes 76
Uncover Your Talents 77
Draw Your Dream Job 78
Color Your Way to Calm:
   Mountain Range 80
Identify Your Values 81
Draw What's in Front of You ... 82
Eat an Elephant (Kind Of) ... 83
Check Off Your Strengths 84
Experiment with Roll
   Breathing 86
Pass the Mic! 87
Be Your Own Best Friend! 88
Draw Your World Without
   Worry 90

Measure Your Growth 91
Mail Your Worries Away 92
Follow This Decision
   Flowchart 94
Discover Your "Don'ts" 95
Enjoy the Highs and Lows 96
Track the Damage 98
Walk the Worry Balance
   Beam 99
Do the Thirty-Day
   Declutter Challenge 100
Color Your Way to Calm:
   Ocean Vibes 102
Test It on the Worry
   B.S. Meter 103
Break It Down! 104
Play Gratitude Bingo 106
Draw Your Anger 107
Do a Worry Word Search 108
Write a Eulogy for Worry 110
Relax with Guided Meditation
   2: All Is Well; All Always
   Will Be 111
Determine Your Control 112
Take a Private Tour Through
   Thoughts and Reality 114
Play Detective 115
Celebrate Your Wins 116
Leave the Baggage Behind ... 118
Relax with Guided Meditation
   3: The Five Senses 119

Leave Clues for Coping 120

Take a Chance on Radical
  Acceptance! 122

Draw Your Sadness 123

See the Glass Half Empty
  and Half Full 124

Turn FOMO Into JOMO! 126

Open Up! 127

Follow Your Finger 128

Color Your Way to Calm:
  Flower Bliss 130

Take Up Space 131

Breathe In Hope 132

Put It on the Shelf 134

Try 4-7-8 Breathing 135

Get Out of Your Own Way ... 136

Keep It—or Lose It! 138

Identify Your Inner Circle 139

Thank Worry 140

Take a Visual Vacation 142

Set a Worry Timer 143

Forget about Yourself! 144

Tap Into Your Wise Mind 146

Put It Down 147

Cash In These Free Freak-
  Out Passes 148

Unwind with Aromatherapy .. 150

Make Your Own Light 151

Unleash Your Inner Warrior! . 152

Relax with Guided Meditation
  4: Let That Stuff Go 154

Follow Your Passion, Not
  Your Fear 155

Take the Scenic Route 156

Fill 'Er Up! 158

Defy Gravity 159

Play "Ten Questions" with
  Worry 160

Stop the Burnout 162

Apply Your Mask! 163

Update Your Status! 164

Color Your Way to Calm:
  Roller-Coaster 166

Swipe Left! 167

Keep an "Almost Missed It!"
  Log 168

Put It on Your Plate 170

Embrace the Butterflies 171

Track Your Body 172

Take Back the Driver's Seat .. 174

Find the Beauty in Being
  Imperfect 175

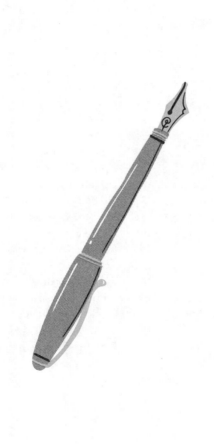

INTRODUCTION

Whatever you are worrying about right now, know this: It's going to be okay! Really. Don't believe me? That's okay too. From personal relationships to work to finances and more, there are a ton of things that might make you worry—and you are not alone in that! Everyone worries from time to time. It's when those worries begin to weigh you down and make living your best life a challenge that a little adjustment is needed.

And that's where we come in! *The No Worries Workbook* is filled with more than 120 creative, easy-to-follow activities that will help you to manage, cope with, and even own your worries—so you can get out of your head and on with your life! You'll:

* Break up with worry once and for all in a heartfelt goodbye letter.
* Follow a road map for getting out of your own way.
* Rearrange your room to gain a new perspective.
* Create an empowering mantra.
* Use a decision tree to distinguish facts from feelings.
* Customize your own self-care checklist.
* And more!

You can work through these activities from beginning to end, or flip through to whatever jumps out at you. This is your journey, so do what feels best for you. Most importantly, as you work through the different activities, remember that you are not a worrier: You are a warrior! The most important tool you have on the path to less worry is your own strength. Even if you don't see yourself as strong now, this book will help you discover your inner power. So are you ready to send those worries packing? Let's get started!

HOW TO USE THIS BOOK

Maybe you are coming to this book after feeling a bit anxious lately. Or maybe you've tried different techniques, online support, or even other books to quell more consistent worry—to no avail. In this case, you may be wondering what makes this book any different. How exactly will reading these pages help in the ways that other resources haven't?

For starters, I understand that the truth about worry is that it isn't "curable." Years of research and interviews in the mental health field have taught me that there is no magic solution that will make it so you never worry about anything ever again. And besides, a little worry can be helpful in certain situations! That urgency you feel when a deadline is looming? If you didn't worry at all, you might blow off getting the job done on time—which unlocks a host of other problems. *The No Worries Workbook* is all about better managing the worries that don't serve you, with the understanding that progress involves a lot of ups and downs, time and practice, and compassion for yourself and your journey to less worry.

In addition, instead of piling on fact after fact and focusing on *why* you worry, this book provides hands-on activities that place the emphasis on what to *do* about it. Each activity is designed to help you cope with your worries in a productive, healthy way so you can get out of your head and on with your life. Of course, you will also be able to explore the causes of your own worries along the way, so you can learn to ease or even prevent future worries. Some activities will refocus your attention away from unproductive thought processes and back to the present moment through physical activity, visualization, and even coloring. Others will involve some deep self-reflection through drawing, filling in the blanks, and more. Each activity comes from the tried-and-true methods I have developed for and discovered from helping my readers, and here I have provided easy instructions, along with more details on how exactly they will help ease your worry.

But before you dive in, there are a few things to remember:

* Have an open mind. Some activities may not seem like a good fit for you, but you should still try each one at least once. You may discover a new, amazing technique for conquering your biggest worry.

* Practice these activities even when you're feeling good. You can't always wait for peak worry mode in order to work your way through this book!

* Be patient with yourself and with the process. Managing worry takes time and practice. Feel the growing pains, and enjoy the ride!

* Take note of the activities that resonate most with you as you work through this book so you can remember what you've learned whenever you feel worried in the future.

Keeping these things in mind as you move through the different activities in the book will make your experience as fun, insightful, and successful as it can be! So, are you ready to worry less and relax more? Let's get started!

ACTIVITIES

Break Up with Worry!

Dear Worry,

Hi, it's _____ (YOUR NAME). I wanted to write and let you know that I'm breaking up with you. And it has nothing to do with you and your ability to stress me out about _____

_____ (YOUR BIGGEST WORRIES).
Nope, it has everything to do with me and the fact that I want better for myself because I deserve it. I've wasted enough time overthinking things that I really can't control, and I refuse to do so any longer.

Sorry, Worry, but I'm stronger than this. Furthermore, I also require a relationship that is give and take, and all you do is take, take, take. You take my time, you take my _____ (SOMETHING ELSE WORRY HAS TAKEN FROM YOU), and I will not allow it anymore. Because I have self-respect. I'm also _____ , _____ , and _____ (THREE OF YOUR BEST ATTRIBUTES)— and someone like me doesn't need to waste any more brain power on you.

I also wanted to let you know that I've grown a lot from you and learned a lot from you. I learned to be resilient, and I also learned _____

_____
(OTHER LESSONS YOU LEARNED FROM WORRY). And for those reasons, I will forever be thankful.

But now, it's time to say goodbye. I wish you all the best.

Never yours again,

_____
(YOUR NAME)

Explore Meditation

You've probably heard about meditation—maybe from a friend who swears by meditating every night, or a coworker who goes to weekly group meditations. So why should you care? And what are the benefits—especially when it comes to combating worry? The following are answers to these questions and more.

WHY SHOULD I MEDITATE?

Studies have shown that meditation can lead to enhanced concentration, lower stress levels, and higher knowledge of yourself. When it comes to worry specifically, meditation helps quiet those overactive thoughts, bringing you back to the present moment.

HOW LONG SHOULD I MEDITATE FOR?

If you're new to meditation, it's recommended that you start with shorter sessions of five to ten minutes. As you grow more comfortable and confident with practice, you can increase the amount of time. Some people find that meditating for a few short periods each day (for example, five-minute meditations at 8 a.m., 12 p.m., and 4 p.m.) is most effective.

IS THERE AN APP FOR THAT?

Of course! In fact, there are tons of options. Headspace and Calm are great for guided meditations that show you the ropes if you are just starting out. Not new to meditation, but looking for background sounds or timers to improve or track your sessions? Check out White Noise and Equanimity.

Rearrange Your Room

You might be surprised at how much a simple change in surroundings can inspire your own inner changes and personal growth. It is a means of self-expression, as well as a productive way to release any worries you might be facing at the moment. Plus, it's just fun!

In this exercise, you're going to rearrange a space in your home. It could be your living room, your bedroom, workspace—whatever! Use the following section to write out any materials you may need, such as paint, new furniture, or organizational items.

SUPPLIES

Now, map out your new space in this grid. Have fun with it and feel your worries fly away!

Make an Anti-Worry Playlist

Music is a powerful tool for rebuffing worries and regulating emotional responses to those worries. In fact, research has shown that music and mood are closely correlated, which explains why those slow, sad songs encourage gloomy feelings, while faster-paced, upbeat tunes make you happier. Create a playlist of all the songs that make *you* happy, so whenever you're feeling stressed or upset, you can simply hit "Play" and leave your worries behind!

My ANTI-WORRY PLAYLIST

1 _____

2 _____

3 _____

4 _____

5 _____

6 _____

Give Yourself a Hand

Sometimes your worries can be linked to feeling a lack of self-worth. And when you're in this period of doubting yourself, it's easy to forget all the great accomplishments you've had in the past. In this activity, you're to list everything you've done lately in the cup. It can be as simple as going in to work when you really wanted to call in sick. You're doing so much better (and more!) than you realize; it's time to own those wins.

EVERYTHING I'VE KICKED BUTT at LATELY

Stop the Spiral! Try One of These Ten Things to Do Instead

Ah, spiraling. It can start with one little thought—then, suddenly, your mind starts spinning until you are totally overwhelmed. Relatable, amirite? Sometimes, the best way to short-circuit this spiral is by doing something else. The following are simple things you can do right this second to bring yourself out of your own mind and back into the present moment.

1   Go for a walk. Take in the scenery, breathe in the fresh air, and look for the beauty that is truly everywhere.

2   Call or text your best friend and ask them about their day. Take the focus off of yourself and put it on someone else.

3   Do one thing you've been putting off for like, ever.

4   Watch your favorite feel-good TV show.

5   Take a twenty-minute nap. Seriously: Sometimes you just need to be a kid again and lie down for a hot second.

6   Dump everything you're thinking into a journal. Getting it down on paper can help get it out of your mind!

7   Teach yourself a new skill.

8   Meditate for five to ten minutes.

9   Watch an inspiring TED Talk. Brenè Brown has an excellent talk called "The Power of Vulnerability."

10 Go to the gym. You don't have to go crazy, just get moving!

NOW,
IT'S YOUR TURN!

In the tornado, write out your
own ideas for things to do
besides spiraling.

Color Your Way to Calm: Mandala

Color your worries away with this fun mandala!

Sip Some Tea

Mindfulness is any practice that brings your focus to the present moment. In turning your awareness to the present, you are shifting it away from any worries about the past or future that might be troubling you.

In this activity, you will use the practice of mindfully drinking tea (or coffee if that's more of your thing) to pull your mind away from worry and back to the here and now. Grounding your thoughts with this easy exercise will allow you to let go of the perceptions and speculations that are not serving you well.

instructions

1   Sit down with a cup of tea or coffee.

2   Hold the cup in your hands and take note of how it feels. What's the texture of the cup? How does the warmth feel on your palms?

3   Take a small sip (once it is cool enough) but don't swallow just yet!

4   Feel the texture and flavor of the beverage in your mouth.

5   Now swallow, and pay attention as the liquid moves down your throat and into your stomach. Really experience the sensations and warmth of it.

6   Continue to mindfully enjoy your drink!

Find Your "It's Okay" Reminders

What is an "It's Okay" reminder? Glad you asked! Essentially, it is a positive affirmation that helps you combat negative thoughts and emotions and feel more optimistic on your path to less worry. These statements are reminders that you are more than capable of handling any obstacles life may throw your way—that everything really *will* be okay, no matter how much you may have been worrying that it won't be.

Following are some great "It's Okay" reminders to try out. Discover which ones resonate the most with you, and make sure they are never out of sight. You can make them your smartphone background, put them in a note on your phone, tape them to your bathroom mirror—wherever you will see them often. This way, when worry strikes, you're able to turn to these truths for comfort and grounding.

I am okay. I always have been, and always will be.

I am more than capable of figuring this out.

Yes, this sucks and will be difficult,
but growth is often born from hardship.

I am enough.

Life is tough, but so am I.

Your turn! Write out your own personalized reminders that will help keep worry away.

1 _____
_____
_____

2 _____
_____
_____

3 _____
_____
_____

4 _____
_____
_____

5 _____
_____
_____

Track Your Location

When you're worrying, you're not living in the present moment. Instead, you're in one of two places: the past or the future. And *of course* spending your time and energy on thoughts about the past or future leads to worry, because these are the two things you have absolutely no control over (no matter how much you try)! What you do have a bit of power over is the present and how you deal with what is happening right now. In this activity, you're going to get in tune with where you are currently: the future, past, or present, so you can become more aware of where your worries take you, and also pull your mind from wherever it may be now back to the present. In the following columns, organize your current worries into the categories of past, future, or present.

PAST	
PRESENT	
FUTURE	

Take Your Ticket for a Worry-Free Day

Sometimes just giving yourself permission to relax, take a breath, and just be is all you need to ease worried thoughts. Copy and carry this ticket with you whenever you need a break from your worries.

MOUNTAIN FOLD

CUT

Get It in Writing!

You are enough. Don't believe me? Fine, I get that; you don't know me. However, you do know yourself. So who better to tackle your worries about your own worth than you?

In this activity, you're going to write a letter to yourself about what you deserve and why. Sound awkward? It may be at first, especially if you've been doubting yourself, but it's an important exercise because you'll be challenging those thoughts head-on. In the following space, you can brainstorm what things you want to include or explore, then use the next page to write your full letter. Flip back to it whenever you need reminding of just how much you deserve.

BRAINSTORM

Dear Me,

Kick FOMO to the Curb

FOMO, or "fear of missing out," has become increasingly common thanks to social media. Day in and day out, you see everything you're missing out on when you turn down plans or make different plans. *Snapchat*, *Instagram*, *Facebook*, and *Twitter* all make sure of that! FOMO can make you feel not only left out and lonely, but also bad about yourself. Worries about falling behind—or being left behind—may start to grow. These thoughts are totally normal, but they're not helpful. When it comes to dealing with FOMO, it's important to reframe being alone as an opportunity to spend time with yourself. In the cell phone, write down some things you can do for fun alone. The next time FOMO strikes, flip to this page and enjoy one (or more) of these activities!

Notes

1 *Whip up a tasty recipe from a favorite cuisine.*

Embrace Uncertainty

Uncertainty is a *huge* trigger for worry. It often opens the door to a host of troubling thoughts, like "What if something terrible happens?" and "I will never be ready for what happens if I can't predict what it will be!" Sometimes, however, the best things in life are what you're unprepared for. They're called surprises, and they can be pretty exciting! In the following space, you're going to fill out an ode to uncertainty that *celebrates* it rather than fears it:

O, Uncertainty,

I used to be so, so _____
(EMOTIONS FELT ABOUT UNCERTAINTY) about your existence.
But now I feel a little more at ease. I even feel

_____ (POSITIVE NEW

EMOTIONS ABOUT UNCERTAINTY) about what you have in
store for me. In fact, some wonderful things have
happened that were unexpected in my life, such as:

_____

_____

_____ .

If I had seen these beautiful moments coming,
maybe I would have been less grateful—less in awe
of them.

So thank you, Uncertainty, because without you,
life would be a lot more boring.

Face Worst-Case Scenarios Head-On

You know those worst-case scenarios you play over and over in your head? The ones that are so good at inflating a small worry into a full-blown panic attack? In the following space, write down every instance that a worst-case scenario did not happen. What was the situation? What did you envision happening? What actually happened? When you're done, go to the next page.

Now, write out all the times that worst-case scenario you worried about *did* happen. Again, what was the situation? What was the scenario that happened?

_____

_____

_____

_____

_____

_____

_____

_____

_____

_____

_____

_____

_____

Compare the two lists: How often did that worst-case scenario happen versus not happen? Most of the time, those end-of-the-world scenarios never actually occur. Maybe the outcome wasn't all that positive—but you made it through! And you probably learned something in the process.

Water Your Growth

Sometimes worry comes from a lack of personal growth or from a fear that you have veered off the path to becoming the best version of yourself. So how exactly are you fostering your growth? In the water droplets above, write down a trait or skill you want to improve on. Then jot down the ways you are currently working toward that goal. If you can't think of anything, you know what your next step is: creating some!

Spin This Decision Wheel

Sometimes it's hard to make a decision on what to do in the moment when you are spiraling into a worried thought. Should you tackle the issue, let it go, leave it for a better time, or step away for a moment to catch your breath? That's where the What Do I Do Right Now? decision wheel comes into play!

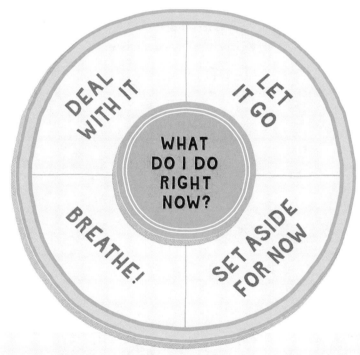

Instructions

Place your pencil or pen on the middle of the wheel. Then spin it! Whatever decision it points to is what you're going to do right now to handle this worry.

Make a Plan

Sometimes when you are worrying about something, it's because you are afraid you won't get through it, and you don't really know how to handle what may come. In this activity, you're going to make a plan for how you're going to own this situation—whatever it may be. Simply acknowledging and accepting what you have control over (and what you don't) can help you focus on what truly needs to be done and to let go of all the rest. With this plan in your arsenal, worry doesn't stand a chance!

1   What am I worried about?

_____

_____

_____

_____

_____

_____

_____

_____

2   Can I control any outcome of this situation?

YES or NO   *(CIRCLE ONE!)*

If no, let it go! If yes...

3   What *can* I control? (For example, the way I react to this situation. The steps I take to clarify any confusion that may be fueling my worry.)

_____

_____

_____

4   What do I need to handle this? (For example, do I need a quiet space? A quick phone call to a friend for support?)

_____

_____

_____

5   Do I need anyone else to help me with this?

_____

_____

_____

6   How did this plan go? Was it helpful in handling this particular situation?

_____

_____

_____

Peer Into This Crystal Ball

A lot of activities for easing worry focus
on turning to the present moment for calmness,
but sometimes looking forward can bring a sense of
peace too, as the future is full of promise! After all,
there is infinite possibility in what hasn't occurred,
right? In the crystal ball above, draw what your ideal
future would look like. Where are you living?
How are you spending your free time?

Appreciate These Ten Beautiful Little Things

When your mind is engulfed in worry, it's difficult to see the truth: that everything is and will be okay. The following are ten little, beautiful things you can appreciate right this second to refocus your mind on the present, easing worry and putting your life into more perspective:

THE SOUNDS of the world around you

THE HAPPY MEMORY of a time when everything felt peaceful and safe

THE SCARS on your heart that show you have cared for something deeply—and will again

THE BODY that carries you through each day

THE SKY overhead

YOUR FAMILY

YOUR FRIENDS

THE FRESH START you woke up to this morning

THE BED you get to come home to each night

THIS MOMENT of awareness you get to experience right now

Look Ahead

What do you have to look forward to? Probably a lot! How about the first sip of a favorite beverage tomorrow morning? Or a fun outing you have marked on your calendar? Or the good friend you haven't met yet? Or the dream job that's waiting around the corner?

Unfortunately, it's easy to get stuck in a feeling of hopelessness when worry has taken hold. So in this activity, you're going to rediscover what the world has to offer by going to the next page and writing down everything you have to look forward to. They can be big things, little things—they just need to spark excitement!

1

2

3

4

5

6

7

8

9

Complete a Self-Care Checklist

When worry has taken the driver's seat, it's easy to throw self-care (all the important things you do for yourself like staying hydrated, getting enough sleep, spending time alone to recharge, and pursuing fun hobbies) out the window. Unfortunately, this only makes things worse, as you don't have the mental or physical energy to combat worry. The following is a self-care checklist designed to help you ensure that you're doing all those little things to care for your mind, body, and soul. Make a copy of this page and check in as needed!

SELF-CARE CHECKLIST

- I slept enough last night
- I brushed my teeth
- I tidied up my living space
- I showered
- I took any and all medications needed
- I took the time to do something I enjoy
- I ate something satisfying and healthy
- I asked for help when I needed it
- I exercised, even if it was just a quick walk
- I drank more than two sips of water today

Connect the Dots

I know it may be hard to believe this when you're in the middle of worrying, but it's going to be okay. Even if the *worst* thing you're thinking of happens, you'll make it through! In this activity, you're going to write each current worry on the lines to the left of the following space. Then you're going to write how that situation is going to be okay on the corresponding lines to the right. Acknowledging your worries while identifying what is realistic and what isn't can be difficult, but learning to do so is crucial for developing more helpful thought patterns and getting out of your own head. Give it your best shot, and keep at it. Over time, you'll find it is easier to do.

CURRENT WORRY	HOW IT WILL BE OKAY
1	
2	
3	

Wake Up with a Mantra

Mantras are great for easing worry because they provide solid support and encouragement to replace negative thoughts. It's a good idea to start your morning with a mantra so those positive vibes are carried through your whole day.

Here are sample morning mantras to try out, followed by space on the next page to write your own!

Today has infinite possibility to be good.

Whatever comes my way, I can and will handle it.

I am bigger than my worries.

This too shall pass.

I am enough.

I am not going to allow a worry to derail
my sense of peace.

I accept that there are things I cannot control.

I release myself of worry today.

The universe will guide me in the right direction.

Endless worry is never effective.

Your turn:

1 _____
  _____

2 _____
  _____

3 _____
  _____

4 _____
  _____

5 _____
  _____

6 _____
  _____

7 _____
  _____

8 _____
  _____

Take Belly Breaths

Belly breathing is a form of deep breathing that helps you relax when worry, stress, or frustration take over. It's also incredibly easy to do! Following are steps for this very simple but effective activity. Bookmark this page for moments when you need to calm down and just *breathe*.

instructions

1   Sit or lie down in a comfortable position.

2   Place one hand on your stomach just below your ribs and the other hand on your chest.

3   Take a deep breath in through your nose and let your belly push your hand outward. Your chest should *not* move.

4   Then breathe out through pursed lips (almost like you're whistling). Notice the hand on your belly move back inward as you exhale.

5   Repeat steps 3 and 4 five to ten times. And remember to take your time!

Draw Your Worries

Just like journaling, drawing can help you get down what you're feeling so you can better sort through the different thoughts and emotions that come with worry. Drawing is also helpful in easing negative emotions, as sometimes all you need is to let it all out— just like venting about a bad workday to a friend! On this page, you're going to draw your worries. What are they? What tangible shape do they take?

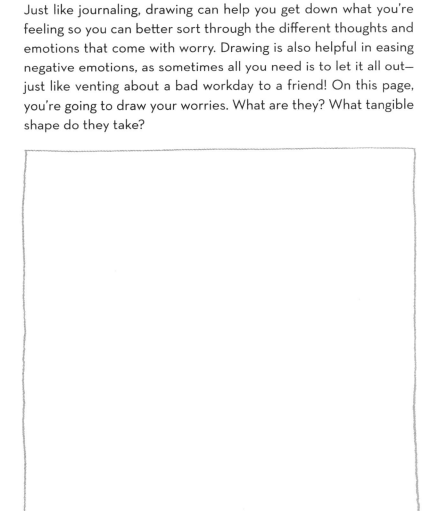

Reroute the Train Wreck of Thought

When you are feeling worried, it's easy for that one fear to multiply into a number of fears and color your perception of, well, pretty much *everything*. For example: "I was late to work this morning because I overslept and there was a huge accident on the freeway. I know I've never been late before and my boss said it was fine, but did she *really* mean it was fine? What if I get *fired*? I'll have to move back in with my parents and *they'll* be disappointed in me. I'll also have to announce it all on *Facebook*, so my peers will judge me too. *What have I done?!!?!*"

Sound familiar? I call this cycle the "Train Wreck of Thought." Your thoughts head down a dreaded path of worry until they completely derail in one large, internal (sometimes external) meltdown. But don't worry (more): There is a great strategy for avoiding this train wreck! That is to take a detour and reroute your thought process toward something more productive. Not sure how to do this? I've created a guided detour for you to fill in. Once you get the hang of it, use it whenever your worries start to steer you toward catastrophe.

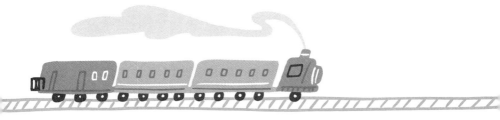

DETOUR

→

Yes, I _____

_____

_____

(YOUR MISTAKE HERE) and I feel

(WHATEVER EMOTION YOU'RE FEELING) about it. But you know what? Everyone makes mistakes. It's part of that whole being human thing I was signed up for. And I did what I needed to do to remedy the situation, such as

_____

_____ *(WAYS YOU HANDLED YOUR MISTAKE).* Next time I'll do better because I was given the opportunity to learn from this!

Look at What's Going *Right*

What's going right in your life right now? Has worry made it a bit difficult to think about the good things? Now's your chance to really focus on the positives life has been giving you! Whether a friend chose you to seek advice from, you made a perfect batch of banana bread, or your boss has been hinting at a promotion lately, looking at and reminding yourself of what is going right can be the perfect way to ease worry—and give it a run for its money.

So get writing!

Draw Your Jealousy

Jealousy is an important emotion to explore when it comes to worry, because jealousy can often be born from those fears of inadequacy—that what you have isn't enough and that someone else will always have it better. As a result, you question yourself, your life...e-v-e-r-y-t-h-i-n-g! So what does jealousy look like to you? By examining this uncomfortable emotion more objectively, you can better describe and understand it—ultimately lessening its power over you.

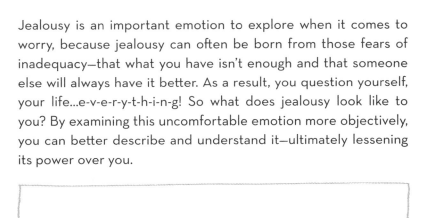

Discover How Worry Is in Your Way

How does worry stand in your way? What does it prevent you from doing? From enjoying? Worry can often frame itself as helpful, promising you that you should be thinking about the things it is telling you—that it is ensuring you are prepared for anything or are in control of a situation. It's time to see worry for what it really is: a roadblock in your journey to confidence, contentment, and success.

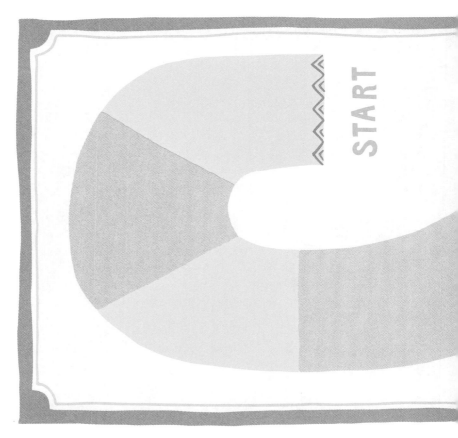

START

In this exercise, you're going to travel along a road map of exactly how a current worry (or one you dealt with recently) is getting in the way of a goal. This goal can be overall happiness, relaxation, self-confidence, success in the workplace—whatever you decide. In each blank space on the map, you'll draw or write out one way this worry is standing in the way of your goal.

GOAL

Pop a Balloon!

Sometimes the best way to defeat a worry is by actually destroying it. This may sound difficult in practice, but a great and easy way to do so is by visualizing yourself popping the worry like a balloon. Through this activity, you take matters into your own hands in order to deliver the fatal *pop*, which can leave you feeling empowered and free from that worry. On each balloon provided, write a worry that is plaguing you right now. Then scribble out the balloon, tap it with your pen or pencil, put a big *x* over it—whatever feels right in order to "pop" it.

Draw Your Happiness

When worry sets in, it can be hard to hold on to good feelings and positive thoughts about your life as it is now. Use this space to remind yourself of all those wonderful things that make you happy by drawing them!

Scribble Your Way to Sleep

Worry likes to creep in just before you go to sleep. A lot of times it may be because you are trying to remember things you have to do the next day, or you're going over things you said or did that day.

This activity is here to help! Every time you can't sleep, write down exactly what's worrying you—or simply what's going through your mind—on these pages. This "brain dump" is a perfect way to get everything out of your head so you can go to sleep.

DATE	WORRIES/THOUGHTS

DATE	WORRIES/THOUGHTS

Color Your Way to Calm: Koi Pond

Swim with the fishes
as your worries
are splashed
away.

Do the Animal ABCs!

One simple strategy for releasing worry is by distracting your mind, forcing it to focus on something else. In this case, it is by listing animal names alphabetically. Sure, it may sound silly and even *too* easy at first, but you'd be surprised how hard it is to remember a worry when you are busy thinking of animals. Starting with "alligator," name one animal for each letter of the alphabet (you can also list them on a separate piece of paper) and watch your worry melt away!

A *lligator*

B

C

D

E

F

G

H

I

J

K

L

M

N

O

P

Q

R

S

T

U

V

W

X

Y

Z

Take a Smaller Step!

The goal of combating worry isn't always to feel 100 percent right away. Sometimes that just isn't realistic. Depending on the amount of worry you feel, plus countless other factors like how much sleep you've had and how busy your workday has been, it can take time. In these cases, it's helpful to focus on feeling a little *less* worried, rather than not worried at all. This takes some of the pressure off, better setting you up for success.

The following are five quick and easy strategies for feeling a little less worried right now. You can also use the space on the next page to brainstorm or keep track of other activities that help make your worries more manageable.

1   Take a quick walk to expel some of the nervous energy.

2   Take a cold shower.

3   Do a face mask or other pampering activity.

4   Scream into a pillow.

5   Write everything you're feeling on a piece of paper, crumple it up, and throw it away.

1

2

3

4

5

Explore the Pros and Cons

Letting go of worry is difficult when it presents itself as helpful. Sure, you're less relaxed and present than you could be, but at least you're in control of the situation and prepared for the worst...right? Well, let's take a closer look at this thought then. What are the benefits of feeding into a current worry you have? What are the disadvantages? It's time to weigh the pros and cons and see if the worry is actually worth it!

PROS	CONS

Unplug!

Social media can be not only a huge time-suck, but also a great instigator for worry. Between the FOMO (fear of missing out) when you see "everyone else" out having a good time, and the endless information at your fingertips, it's easy to walk away from a web-surfing session feeling anxious and pessimistic. Need a little more before you're willing to put your phone down for the next twenty-four hours? The following are the top five reasons why unplugging from social media for a day can help you cope with or even prevent worry:

1 You will notice the things you wouldn't have seen if you were busy staring at your phone.

2 You will connect with others in real life more.

3 You will avoid FOMO.

4 You will have more time to spend doing something you enjoy.

5 You will be able to redirect your focus from the past to the present.

Discover Your Purpose

Sometimes worry can stem from a fear that you aren't living a purposeful life. Maybe, after scrolling through everyone's highlight reel of achievements on *Instagram* or hearing about a friend or family member's recent success, you start to doubt that you are doing *anything* worthwhile. So what do you do? Aside from giving yourself more credit (which you should still do!), it can help to create a statement of your purpose that you can read back to yourself whenever you start to worry about whether you are taking the right steps, or when you worry that your behavior lately might not align with your goals.

Use the space on this page to write out what your beliefs are. On the next page, write down what makes you feel accomplished, and what makes you happy. You can even ask others what they believe their purpose is, for inspiration.

My PURPOSE

MY BELIEFS

1 _____

2 _____

3 _____

4 _____

5 _____

THINGS THAT MAKE ME FEEL ACCOMPLISHED

1
2
3
4
5

THINGS THAT MAKE ME HAPPY

1
2
3
4
5

Brainstorming my purpose...

Relax with Guided Meditation 1: BREATHE IN CALM; EXHALE HOPE

Meditation is the wonderful art of calming overactive thoughts and refocusing your mind on the present moment. Guided meditations are especially great for easing worry, as they offer more assistance in focusing a frantic mind. In this guided meditation, you're going to breathe your way to a calm, hopeful state by first recording yourself reading the following steps, then playing the recording back to yourself to complete the meditation.

instructions

1   Sit in a comfortable position in a quiet, safe space.

2   Take a deep, intentional breath in through your nose. As your lungs fill with air, feel a sense of calm travel through your body. Notice your chest expand, filling with relaxation. Observe your muscles lessening their tension.

3   Exhale through your mouth while visualizing the idea of hope. What does hope look like? What possibilities are you expelling into the universe as you breathe out now?

4   Repeat steps 2 and 3 and feel the worry melt away.

Send a Text

If your worry could text you about a situation you're currently stressing over, what would it say? Probably a lot of things that make it worse, right? For example: "You're never going to figure this out!" and "You ruin everything." What if you could stop it in its tracks with a text or two of your own? You can, and that's just what you're going to do here! In the space provided, shut down your worry's text by letting it know that everything is going to work out (and why). And if worry tries to text back with more of the same old panic, make your word final by leaving it on "read."

Map Out Your Future Self

Sometimes worry can come from a fear that you aren't living up to your full potential. Maybe hours of scrolling through *Instagram*, *Facebook*, or *Twitter* have you wondering if there is anything to feel proud of in your own life. It's a perfectly normal thing to worry about, but the truth is that you still have time—and lots of it—to become who it is that you want to be. And this activity is here to help you along the way!

Here, you're going to create a plan for becoming your ideal future self, so you can stop worrying and start working toward concrete goals. First, use the following lines to brainstorm what your ideal future self is. Then use the following sections to create your plan of action:

My ideal future self is:

_____

_____

_____

_____

_____

_____

_____

_____

_____

_____

_____

My FUTURE SELF *in Action*

SKILLS NEEDED TO BECOME IDEAL SELF

	skill	*how to attain*
1		
2		
3		
4		
5		

THINGS NEEDED TO BECOME IDEAL SELF

	person/material	*how to attain*
1		
2		
3		
4		
5		

DEADLINES FOR IDEAL SELF

	skill/person/material	*when I hope to attain this by*
1		
2		
3		
4		
5		

Take a "Walk"

Like meditation, visualization is a great mindfulness exercise that can refocus your thoughts away from worry and on the present moment. In this scenario, you will be imagining walking down a spiral staircase. Of course, it's not always easy to do right away, so I have provided this drawing to help you get started. Follow the illustration slowly with your eyes, from the top to the bottom. Then close your eyes and picture it in your mind. You can add textures to the steps, a temperature to the stairwell—anything that adds to the visual as you imagine yourself walking down it.

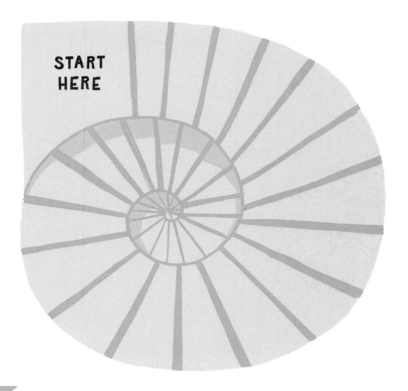

START
HERE

Write a Letter to Future You

You know what you need to hear most when you're worried—so get it down on paper! This way, you will have those perfect calming words at the ready when you're in the middle of a worried thought (or major freak-out). Use the following template to write your letter to your future, worrying self. Be sure to fill it with the compassionate, understanding, and hopeful words that will help you feel less worried.

Dear _____ (YOUR NAME),

_____

_____

_____

_____

_____

_____

_____

_____

_____

Love,

_____
(YOUR NAME)

Rewrite the Story You Tell Yourself

The story you tell yourself—a.k.a. negative self-talk about things like your intelligence or your looks—can have a huge impact on the way you view your life *and* yourself. After all, when the voice inside your head is constantly telling you something (like you aren't good enough), it's hard not to believe it after a while.

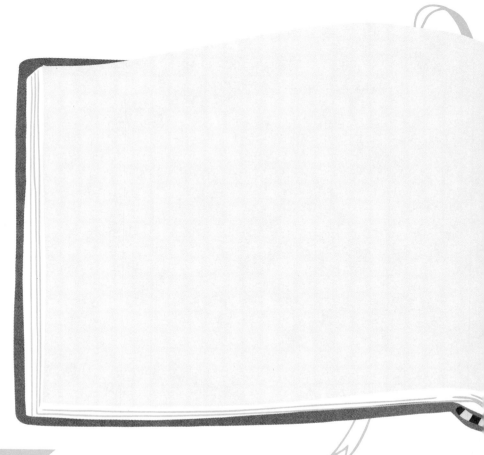

In this activity, you're going to be rewriting an unhelpful narrative that may be causing you worry right now. On the left page of this open book, write your current story. On the right page, rewrite that story in a kinder, more positive way. If you aren't sure how, try challenging any negativity in the story on the right. What is backing up those negative beliefs?

Give Thanks

You are never alone. At every step of the way there are people who are ready and willing to help you—all you need to do is ask. It's important to remember that it's okay to ask for this help, and it can even set you up for more success when it comes to future stressors. This activity serves as your reminder of this fact. Use the following space to write a thank-you letter to someone who has helped you along the way. It can be a parent, friend, or even a kind stranger.

Dear _____ *(THEIR NAME)*,

_____

_____

_____

_____

_____

_____

_____

_____

_____

Sincerely,

_____

(YOUR NAME)

Ride the Wave

Sometimes your best bet for handling worry is by simply going with the flow. You may have heard this before, and yes, it *is* easier said than done, but never fear: This mindful exercise will make it a bit easier—and literal! Slowly trace a finger along the waves on this page, from left to right. Repeat from right to left and back again until you feel your worries fading into the background. It may seem too simple to work at first, but this mindful, meaningful task is a great way to get out of your head and into the present moment.

Rediscover the Real You

When you're consumed with worry, it's easy to feel that this is how you always are—a stressed-out, overwhelmed worrier. But it isn't! This activity will help you reconnect with who you are deep down, so you can tackle your worries with more confidence and strength.

ITEMS NEEDED: A jar   Ten to twenty small strips of paper

Instructions

1. Write one positive trait about yourself on each slip of paper, then fold the slips in half.

2. Place the folded papers in the jar and put the jar somewhere easily accessible, like your desk or bedside table.

3. The next time you feel like all you are is a worrier, pull out a piece of paper and read the trait written on it.

4. Whatever trait you drew, focus on practicing it now. For example, maybe it was "resilience." Focus on looking at any disappointment or challenge big or small that has come your way (or may in the near future) in a more positive light. What opportunities does it offer?

5. You can use the next page to brainstorm some of your traits before creating your Real You jar!

I am...

Cross Out Your Mistakes

Everyone makes mistakes. It's a part of life! Sometimes, though, it can be hard to take this truth to heart. Instead, rumination follows, and you get stuck in a cycle of self-criticism and doubt. This activity is here to help you let go of these mistakes once and for all. Write out the mistakes you're currently struggling with in the following boxes. Then cross them out! You are still acknowledging that you messed up, but you're also giving yourself permission to let go and move on.

Uncover Your Talents

Worry can often come from a fear of inadequacy—of not being "enough." Even if you know deep down that it isn't true, it can be hard to beat out those little voices of self-doubt during a moment of worry. In this exercise, you're going to write everything you're good at—big *and* small—to challenge those B.S. reasons your worries may have come up with to "prove" you aren't enough.

I am great at...

_____

_____

_____

_____

_____

_____

_____

_____

_____

_____

_____

_____

_____

_____

_____

Draw Your Dream Job

Work worry is a huge stressor for a lot of people. Sometimes this worry is the product of not liking what you're doing. Maybe you feel like you are stuck in a career that you thought was the right fit, but now know isn't, and you worry you will never get out. Does this sound like you? Then it's time to get proactive! Ask yourself the following questions to start really thinking about your dream job. Write your answers in the space provided.

* What setting do you work in now? An office? An outdoor site? How do you feel about it? What could be better?
* What don't you like about your current job position? Is there an element missing that you want in a future job—more client interaction or perhaps more independence or flexibility?
* How are your coworkers now? Do you enjoy working with them? What kind of relationship do you want going forward with coworkers?
* When you close your eyes and think about your ideal job title, responsibilities, and setting, what comes to mind?

Next, explore your answers and other thoughts from your brainstorming in more detail by drawing them out in the space provided. This exercise is a great way to express everything you might be thinking about your dream job—including the things you may not have thought of before but that have now come to mind as you dump everything onto the page. Feel your dreams start to take a concrete shape now!

Color Your Way to Calm: Mountain Range

Scale these mountains with your favorite colored pencils, and feel your worry evaporate!

Identify Your Values

Worry can sometimes come from feeling like you aren't living your life the way you should be. And that's often because you aren't operating according to your values. For example, maybe family's important to you, but you've been neglecting that quality time lately, and you end up feeling lonely or unfulfilled. So what are your values? And how are you living according to them? In the following left column, write down what you value (friends, religion, self-care, etc.). Then, in the right column, write down how you're abiding by each of these. Can't come up with an answer? It's time to make an adjustment in your life!

MY VALUES	HOW I'M PRACTICING THEM

Draw What's in Front of You

Like meditation and visualization, drawing is a great mindfulness exercise that pulls your focus away from worry and on to the physical action you are doing. In this activity, you're going to draw exactly what's in front of you. Maybe it's a coffee table with books stacked on top of it, an open window to the backyard, or a cup of hot coffee—draw away!

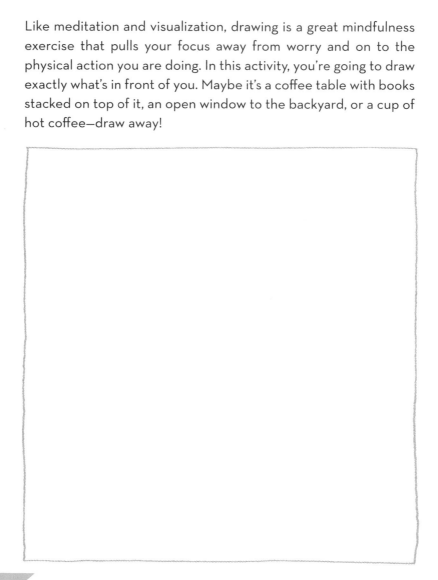

Eat an Elephant (Kind Of)

How do you eat an elephant? Piece by piece, as the saying goes! Sometimes worry can come from taking on a task that feels overwhelming. How will you ever get this done on time? By keeping that elephant in mind: one little piece at a time. And this activity is here to help you do just that. Choose a task you need to complete, then label the different sections of the elephant here with smaller tasks you will need to do in order to finish that bigger project. Then get to work on one little "piece." As you complete each smaller task, color in that part of the elephant until there is nothing left to color.

Check Off Your Strengths

You are more capable than you realize; I promise you this. As a Grade A Worrier myself, I know how it feels to doubt yourself relentlessly. But I also know what it's like to prove yourself wrong. Of course, it can still be difficult to believe in yourself when you get stuck in a spiral of worried thoughts. Luckily, this activity is here to help! Here are the top ten signs that you are capable of overcoming whatever life (and worry) throws at you. Whenever you are in doubt, turn to this checklist and mark the ways that you can do this (whatever "this" may be)!

STRENGTHS
CHECKLIST

- [ ] You got out of bed today, even though you may have wanted to hide under the covers until the day passed.

- [ ] You've handled things like this before. Possibly far worse, even. Really difficult situations that tested and challenged you. It wasn't fun, but you made it through.

- You were compassionate even when it may have been hard and you felt entitled to be anything but.

- You have had difficult conversations with friends, family, coworkers, even strangers when you would rather not, knowing that it was necessary. And you got through it!

- You met deadlines you may have thought you'd never meet.

- You've proven your worries wrong, accomplishing a goal you told yourself you'd never reach.

- You have made mistakes—possibly a *lot* of mistakes—but you learned from them! You found the beauty and value in these lessons, even when it hurt a little (or a lot).

- You've had your heart broken but haven't closed it to future happiness.

- You've said "No" when you needed to even if it was hard. You have limitations, but this isn't a failure. It's just reality.

- You've allowed yourself to take breaks when you need them. You understand (or are at least beginning to understand) the value of taking a step back and saying, "I need a minute to breathe."

Experiment with Roll Breathing

Roll breathing is a great mindfulness exercise that redirects your focus to the rhythm of your breaths and away from your current worries. As you step away from overwhelming thoughts to breathe, it becomes easier to let go of what is troubling you. In this guided meditation, you are going to breathe your way to a more relaxed state by first recording yourself reading the following steps, then playing the recording back to yourself to complete the meditation.

instructions

1   Sit in a comfortable position in a quiet place, and place your left hand on your stomach and your right hand on your chest.

2   Inhale through your nose and feel the air filling your lower lungs so that your left hand rises but your right hand remains still.

3   Exhale slowly through your mouth.

4   Repeat steps 2 and 3 eight to ten times.

5   Now start to inhale through your nose into your lower lungs again, then shift your breathing to inhale into your upper chest so that your right hand is pushed out.

6   Exhale slowly through your mouth, making a soft whooshing sound as your left and then right hands move back inward. Notice the tension leaving your body as you exhale.

7   Repeat steps 5 and 6 eight to ten more times. Note: Some people may become dizzy after their first time trying this, so stand up slowly afterward!

Pass the Mic!

It might seem counterintuitive at first, but sometimes the best way to see a worry for what it is (irrational and unhelpful) is by giving it the space to run its course. Okay, your boss is mad at you: so what? What is your worry saying will happen next? After that? As you let the worry take center stage and write down what it is saying, you'll be able to see for yourself just how ridiculous and harmful worries can be. Pass the mic to your worry now and record what it says here:

Worry: _____

_____

which means _____

_____

and then _____

_____

which will mean _____

_____

and then _____

_____

Be Your Own Best Friend!

Social worker Brenè Brown once said, "Talk to yourself like someone you love." In other words, if you wouldn't say something to your best friend, don't say it to yourself! Being compassionate toward yourself is especially important when it comes to reducing worry in your daily life, because worry is often the product of negative self-talk. For example, those mean things you say to yourself when you make a mistake or don't do something perfectly lead into worries about inadequacy and failure. Practicing kindness and patience with yourself can be difficult at times, of course, especially if you are so used to critiquing everything you do, which is why you are going to start here by writing a letter to yourself as if it were to a best friend. You will be able to give yourself a little of the love you deserve, and also pick up more on how differently you may be treating yourself versus the people closest to you. Use the template on the following page to write your letter.

Dear _____ (YOUR NAME),

Hi, it's _____ (YOUR NAME). We
need to talk. No, I'm not mad or anything—don't
worry! I just think you need a bit of a pep talk
since you've been super stressed lately about that
thing. You know... _____

_____
_____ (A SPECIFIC WORRY).
You need to remember to be _____

_____
(E.G., KIND, PATIENT, HOPEFUL) toward yourself, because
life is already difficult enough without you harping
on yourself 24/7! Listen, I know you could have
done "better" or "more," but hey: you didn't. And
that's okay, because you're human! You only can
do so much. And honestly? What you *did* do is the
best you could at that moment. And you can't ask
more from yourself.

    You deserve to be _____

_____
(E.G., HAPPY, LESS STRESSED), and more. Please don't
forget that.

Love,

_____
(YOUR NAME)

Draw Your World Without Worry

What would your world look like without worry? Does it feel way out of reach? Well, you're going to get a little closer to that world now! Here you will explore a worry-free reality through the mindful practice of drawing. Getting this vision down on paper lets you cultivate more hope in your journey to less worry, while learning more about what exactly you want in life that worry has held you back from.

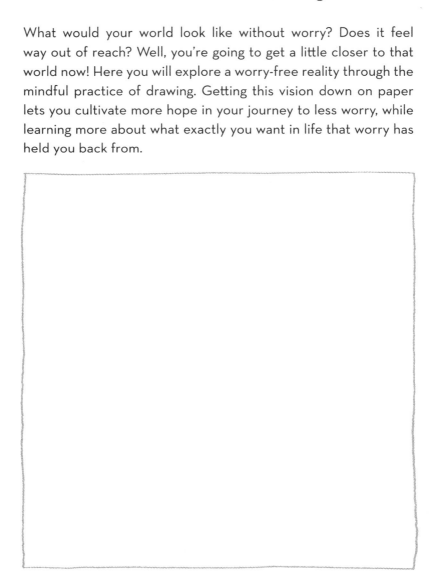

Measure Your Growth

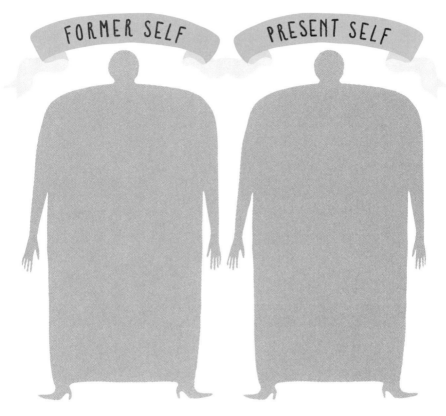

FORMER SELF

PRESENT SELF

When worry becomes overwhelming, it's important to remember that it gets better. It always does, doesn't it? Just look how much you've grown! Actually, that's what you're going to do here. More specifically, you're going to describe two versions of yourself: who you were two years ago and who you are today. You're going to write or draw your habits, fears, hobbies, job—everything that encases who you were then and who you are now—in the figures here. Then look at the differences.

Mail Your Worries Away

Sometimes all it takes to reclaim your power over a worry is a quick, hands-on experience that makes you feel more in control. In this activity, you're going to mail the worries that aren't serving you far away so you can take back that power. On each postcard provided, write out what you're worrying about right now, then address each one to a destination (as specific or vague as you would like, from that abandoned house you grew up next to, to a state or country thousands of miles from home).

to:

from:

to:

from:

Follow This Decision Flowchart

Let it go, or deal with it? That is the question that often keeps you from getting past pesky worries. Fortunately, this decision tree is here to help you answer it once and for all! With each worry you're faced with right now, follow the questions in the flowchart here to find out whether you should let it go or if it is a legitimate concern that you should deal with head-on.

IS THIS SOMETHING THAT I AM WORRIED *MIGHT* HAPPEN OR IS IT SOMETHING THAT IS *ACTUALLY* GOING TO HAPPEN?

MIGHT HAPPEN

ACTUALLY WILL HAPPEN

LET IT GO!

ARE THERE THINGS I CAN DO TO MAKE IT BETTER?

YES

NO

DEAL WITH IT!

LET IT GO!

Discover Your "Don'ts"

There are a number of things you definitely *shouldn't* do when worrying: things that can turn a small thought into a meltdown, or at least keep the flame of a worry burning strong. Like drinking seven cups of coffee in an hour, or scrolling through your ex's Venmo activity. Take some time now to identify what makes things worse for you when you're worried. Not sure where to start? Think about a past scenario where your worry quickly went from 0 to 100. What accelerated that freak-out? Whenever you feel yourself beginning to worry, turn back to this page as a reminder of what to avoid to keep the situation more manageable until you can let go of the worry for good.

Enjoy the Highs *and* Lows

In life—and more specifically in your journey to less worry—there will be highs and lows: peaks where you feel at peace and in control of your worry, and valleys where overwhelming thoughts seem to have the reins while you are just along for the ride. Learning to accept the bad with the good is an important part of getting through that ride in one piece. Plus you may also find that accepting the lows in your journey is actually helpful in easing some of your worry! It's true: Worry can often come from a need for control, as well as the self-inflicted pressure for things to always be great. By releasing some of this control and removing the weight of that pressure from your shoulders, you may find yourself feeling less worried.

In this activity, you will kick-start your path to accepting all those highs and lows by labeling the illustration on the next page. On each mountaintop, write down something that's going well for you right now. In each valley, write down something you wish could change or that you're unhappy with at this moment.

Track the Damage

Does your worry ever feel like a tornado of thoughts that gets faster and faster until you feel like you've lost all control of your own mind? I call it "the spiral," and it can tear quite a path through your life. So what does your spiral suck up? Most likely a lot: your time, energy, and peace of mind, just to name a few. In this exercise, you're going to dive deeper into the destruction that your spiral of worry creates by writing down everything it sucks up in the tornado above. Seeing the destruction in more detail serves as a reminder of how ineffective and damaging your worries can be, so you can finally let them go.

Walk the Worry Balance Beam

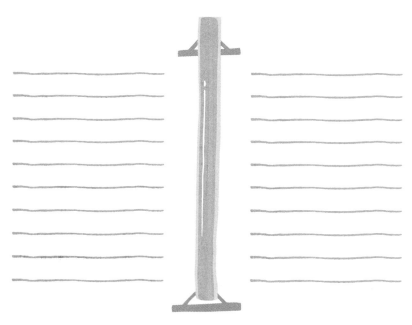

Life is all about balance: work time versus personal time; alone time versus time with loved ones. Often when you're in a place of worry, it's from a lack of balance in one or more aspects of your life. In this activity, you're going to determine what balance looks like to you—what things matter when you think about this concept. On either side of the balance beam above, sort out the things that are important to your life. Pair the opposites across from one another—for example, taking care of others versus taking care of yourself, or work versus play—and fill in the opposites that are remaining (everything needs a counterweight!). When putting everything into perspective in this way, you can identify what things you need to focus on and what might be out of balance.

Do the Thirty-Day Declutter Challenge

There is a theory that I like to call the "Messy Room Conundrum." Over the course of weeks, months, and years, your bedroom can get a bit messy. It happens! However, the messier your bedroom becomes, the messier your mind becomes as well. Think about it: Just how calm can you be when you are digging through piles of belongings to find a clean shirt for work? And of course, the more chaotic your mind becomes in this mess, the more chaotic your bedroom will be, as you start to feel unable to tackle this mounting clutter. It becomes a vicious cycle—and that's where the Thirty-Day Declutter Challenge comes into play. For each day of this challenge, you will target one category of items, tossing out the clutter until you have created a peaceful space where you can cultivate a more peaceful mind. As you complete each category, check off the box on the following chart.

My DECLUTTER
CHALLENGE CHECKLIST

- Old school papers
- Shoes that are falling apart
- Clothes you bought for a day that never happened
- Outdated electronics
- Books you never read (and never *will* read)
- Broken or untouched DVDs
- Expired medications
- Jewelry you never wear
- Get your inbox to 0 (or less than 27,000)
- Old makeup
- Old skin-care products
- Random, unused accessories
- Old magazines
- Broken appliances
- Old food containers

- Unused decorations
- Old/expired cleaning supplies
- Never-been-used items in that junk drawer
- Old bathing suits
- Multiples of items
- Receipts for small or discarded items
- Old mail
- Old paperwork
- Unused holiday decorations
- Old underwear
- Expired or unused travel items
- Gifts you kept out of guilt
- Old desk supplies
- Old craft supplies
- Broken dishes, cups, utensils, etc.

Color Your Way to Calm: Ocean Vibes

Float along in this expansive ocean
as your worries are washed away!

Test It on the Worry B.S. Meter

There is a *lot* of B.S. involved in worry! After all, worry tends to convince you that bad things are going to happen—things that probably never do. It robs you of the present moment, and puts you in an alternate dimension where everything is bad. In this activity, you're going to explore which worries may be valid—and which ones may be B.S. First, take a pencil and lay it flat over the meter provided. This will act as your gauge. As you think about a current worry, ask yourself these questions to determine whether it is B.S. or not: Do I have any evidence that this worry holds truth? Am I freaking out as a distraction from putting in the work? Move the pencil to the appropriate space on the gauge as you answer the questions.

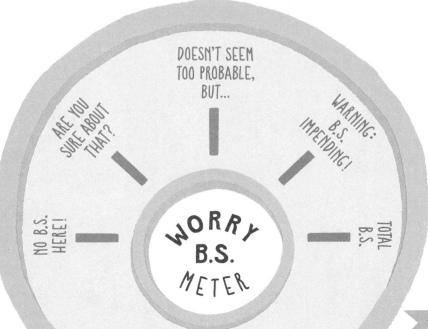

Break It Down!

When you have a huge project in front of you, it can be hard to figure out where to even start. So many things to do, people to talk to, decisions to make—it's a lot! And worry-inducing at that. Fortunately this activity is here to help you get things done and squash your worries by breaking larger tasks down into more manageable, bite-sized pieces that you feel ready to take on. On each stair on the next page, write down one small step required to complete a larger task on your plate. Think about things in terms of the most basic actions you will need to do, like calling a client for a price range or editing a review for grammar. Then get to it—one step at a time! You can copy this template and use it with any large task.

Play Gratitude Bingo

Gratitude is excellent at diminishing worry, because it draws your focus away from what is "wrong" (or what your worries are telling you is wrong) and toward what is "right" (what you can be thankful for in this moment). While some people like writing things out, others are more visual, so I've created a gratitude bingo game that will give you examples of what you can be grateful for now, so you can mark off the good things in your life.

GRATITUDE

FAMILY	FRIENDS	MONEY IN THE BANK
AN EDUCATION	WI-FI	FREE SPACE (WRITE YOUR OWN)

BINGO

Draw Your Anger

What does anger look like to you? Is there something making you angry right now? A part of worry is the uncomfortable emotions that come with it—emotions like anger and frustration, maybe at yourself for worrying or at the situation you're worried about. Drawing out your anger is a great way to address this emotion and figure out where it is coming from. By expressing and labeling how you feel, the strength of this powerful emotion's hold on you lessens.

Do a Worry Word Search

It's time to get back to the basics with a word search! In this activity, you're going to find the following words in the word search on the next page. This fun puzzle is an easy way to reroute your thoughts away from worry as you try to find each of the words.

BREATHE

INHALE

EXHALE

ACCEPTANCE

PEACE

OCEAN

LOVE

CALM

REALITY

RELAX

Q	N	Z	S	G	P	A	L	E	R
E	S	K	B	L	S	I	Z	O	E
X	M	B	R	A	I	N	H	C	A
H	I	L	E	X	J	H	N	E	L
A	G	O	A	Q	O	A	A	Y	I
L	P	C	T	C	T	L	E	N	T
M	O	X	H	P	J	E	C	I	Y
C	A	V	E	F	E	N	O	D	T
W	Q	C	E	X	Z	A	K	P	I
P	C	Y	I	A	H	P	C	O	L
A	B	V	O	L	G	A	U	E	V
Z	S	G	Z	E	O	Q	L	M	U
H	T	A	E	R	B	S	J	E	R

Write a Eulogy for Worry

It's time to lay worry to rest—literally. In this activity, you're going to get a little creative as you write a eulogy for your worry so you can let go of whatever thoughts have been troubling you! Read it out loud when you're finished for an extra boost of empowerment.

Here lies Worry:

A friend, a foe, and, most importantly, a teacher. Worry taught me a lot about myself. For example, I will never forget when Worry schooled me in

_____

_____

(A LESSON WORRY TAUGHT YOU), or when it _____

_____

_____

(A SECOND LESSON LEARNED). Worry and I have been through a lot—like the time _____

_____

_____

(MEMORY OF A WORRY).

We didn't think we'd make it through, but we did. We really did. I will never forget you, Worry.

Rest easy.

Relax with Guided Meditation 2:
ALL IS WELL; ALL ALWAYS WILL BE

Meditation is a great way to calm worried thoughts and bring yourself back to the present moment. Sometimes, though, it can be hard to sit still and just *be*. This is where guided meditation comes in. In guided meditation, you're led through a mindful practice, typically by a teacher, meditation group leader, or voice recording. In this case, you're going to record yourself reading the following steps, then play the recording back to yourself to complete the meditation.

instructions

1   Sit in a comfortable position in a quiet, safe space.

2   Take a deep breath in through your nose. Feel as you sink into yourself and this moment.

3   Exhale.

4   Breathe in again. Think about the things you can't control.

5   Breathe out, allowing yourself to let go of these things.

6   As you breathe in once more, take in everything you feel you have done wrong, everything you're fearful will go wrong.

7   Now breathe it out, slowly and carefully. Realize that all is well and all always will be.

Determine Your Control

There are some things you can control in life...and a *lot* of things you definitely can't! Unfortunately, worry likes to tell you otherwise, and soon you are convinced that obsessing over a situation can actually help—somehow. It's time to nip that thought in the bud once and for all! In this activity, you're going to determine what

WHAT I CAN CONTROL

1   My reaction to a problem

things you actually can control and what things you *can't* control. As you list things in each column, consider what things in the "What I Can't Control" list you have been trying to control lately. This exercise will help you focus on what you can actually do and accept what things you need to let go of.

WHAT I CAN'T CONTROL

1   What my coworker thinks

Take a Private Tour Through Thoughts and Reality

Is a current worry just a thought? Or does it represent the reality of a situation? It can be difficult to tell in the moment, which is why this activity will guide you through an examination of thoughts versus reality. In each cloud, write down something you're worried about. Then, in the lines below that cloud, describe the facts you have about the actual situation. Do they match up with your worry? If not, write, "Just a thought!" beside the cloud. I've given an example to get you started.

I'm never going to get this homework assignment done!!!

Just a thought

Play Detective

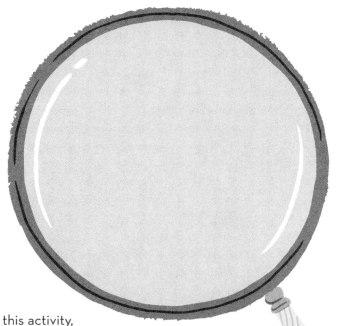

In this activity,
you're going to be
playing detective to determine whether there
is evidence to support a worry you are having.
In the magnifying glass, write out the clues that
this worry is worth paying attention to. For example,
maybe you're worried that your boss is mad at you.
Have you been hitting your deadlines? Not exactly...
Have you been late to work? Sometimes... If you can't
come up with any real evidence (your deadlines have
been met, you've gotten to work on time, etc.), you know
it's time to file that case away!

Celebrate Your Wins

The path to less worry is full of ups and downs, just like any other important journey you will go through in life. Sometimes you may have a day or week or maybe month where you feel completely overcome with worry at every turn. And it's disheartening, to say the least. You may feel like every time this happens you're jumping back to square one, but that isn't true! Progress isn't a straight line upward—and it's time to remind yourself of that by looking at all the strides you have made with your worries. In each of the stars, write down every accomplishment you have had—big *and* small—on the road to reducing worry. These can include everything from getting a promotion to making it to work on time and still managing to grab some Starbucks on the way. It's an easy, empowering way to put your journey, and *yourself*, into perspective.

Leave the Baggage Behind

In order to move forward and let go of worry, you need to leave some of the extra baggage behind. This baggage may be in the form of a toxic friendship or the memory of a job you were fired from years ago. In this activity, you're going to determine what should be let go by "packing" for your future. Inside the suitcase, write or draw the experiences, skills, people, etc. you absolutely want to bring with you. Now, what is left? What things could you make room for in the suitcase, and what things would simply weigh you down? Write these things on the lines provided.

Relax with Guided Meditation 3:
THE FIVE SENSES

Guided meditation is a great way to tune back into the present moment and out of worried thoughts. Despite what many want to think, multitasking—especially effective multitasking—is very difficult, if not impossible, so giving your mind something to do makes it hard for nagging thoughts to keep nagging. An easy meditation to try is one in which you tune in to the five senses by thinking about your surroundings as they relate to each one. Next to each sense, write down the world as it is, right this second. For example: "I am sitting on a chair. I **feel** the chair on my back. I **hear** birds chirping and **smell** freshly cut grass. I **taste** my dinner I just ate. I **see** the sun setting."

Leave Clues for Coping

When you're in a worry-free state of mind, it's a great idea to leave hints for the future freaking-out you. After all, your psyche is a lot clearer during these states, which leaves plenty of space and positivity for great ideas to grow in. These hints will give you the information you need to cope the next time worry strikes. They can include tips like going for a quick walk, taking a really cold shower, or writing down positive affirmations that make you feel empowered. Write down your hints on the bread crumbs that follow.

Take a Chance on Radical Acceptance!

Radical acceptance is the practice of allowing the things that you can't control or don't like to simply exist as they are without resisting. Sounds difficult, right? Fortunately, this activity will make it a little easier to do. Here you're going to write down statements of acceptance to repeat to yourself in times of distress. These words will remind you that the thing you're faced with can't be controlled, and that accepting this will help you get through with less worry. Here are a couple of sample radical acceptance statements to get you started:

What will be, will be.

It is what it is.

Your turn:

Draw Your Sadness

Sadness is an important emotion to explore when it comes to worry, because when you are in a spiral of worry it can often feel like a storm that will never pass. On top of the worry itself, you start to feel more and more disheartened. So, what things make you feel down in the dumps? Mindfully drawing out this emotion not only creates a release from any sadness you might have felt recently; it can also help you identify how sadness might be linked to your own worries, past or present. By labeling and describing how you feel, the strength of this emotion's hold on you can be lessened.

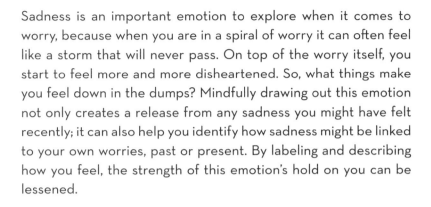

See the Glass Half Empty *and* Half Full

The good and the bad can coexist, no matter what your worries may say. Sometimes the glass is half empty *and* half full—and sometimes you're dealing with a few half-empty glasses and a few half-full ones. What matters is that you come to terms with this balance in life, so it can become one fewer thing you worry about.

WHAT IF I CAN'T MAKE THIS DEADLINE?

I'll need to ask my boss for an extension.

I'll know to set aside more time in the future so it won't happen again!

This activity can help you do just that. Above each glass, write down a worry. Inside the glass, write the half-full truth of that worry in the top portion and the half-empty truth of the worry in the bottom portion. Then take a deep breath, and remember: It's the balance of life!

Turn FOMO Into JOMO!

You probably know about FOMO (fear of missing out) by now, but have you heard of its opposite, the wonderful JOMO? JOMO, or the *joy* of missing out, is a mind-set that celebrates those opportunities you get to spend alone. It's all about appreciating what you do have (for example, the chance to recharge with a lush bubble bath) and letting go of what you don't (like a fancy drink at the swanky club a friend just posted about on *Instagram*). In this exercise, you're going to write down moments that usually give you instant FOMO, then flip things around to figure out how those FOMO moments can actually be JOMO moments.

FOMO   JOMO

Open Up!

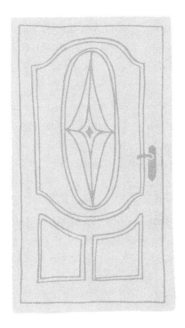 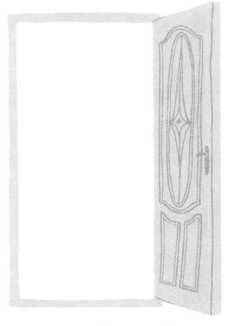

You know the phrase well: "When one door closes, another one always opens." Cliché? Sure. True? Absolutely. Every ending has to be followed by a new beginning eventually, and beginnings are full of potential! For example, let's say you're going through a break-up. It's painful, yes, but maybe it also paves the way for a better focus on self-care. In this activity, you're going to reframe something that you have always viewed as one of those "closed doors" as the opening of a *new* door. Start by writing down that missed opportunity or ending in the closed door. Then use the space in the open door to think about the new start that has come (or will come) from it. It's time to recognize that yes, things can end, and it hurts, but it's an opportunity for something better.

Follow Your Finger

Are you in the present, the past, or the future? When you are stuck in worried thoughts, you are usually existing in either the past or the future, neglecting the here and now. It's time to get back to the present, and this easy activity is here to help!

On the next page, place your finger on or under the word "Present." This is where you will always want to end up. Let your mind wander now. Think about what is happening around you—what you may be hearing, seeing, feeling, etc. When you notice your thoughts shifting to a worry, move your finger accordingly to indicate whether that worry belongs in the past or the future. To work your way back to the present, gently invite yourself to the "present" section by moving your finger to the middle of the page and again addressing the current moment.

PAST

PRESENT

FUTURE

Color Your Way to Calm: Flower Bliss

Stop to smell the flowers,
and watch as your worries drift away.

Take Up Space

Experts say that the average person has anywhere from sixty to eighty thousand thoughts *per day*. That's a lot of thinking! And a lot of opportunity for worry to sneak in... In this activity, you're going to fill up that space so worry has no room to join in! In the brain on this page, draw or write about the kinds of thoughts and emotions you think would serve you better than worry.

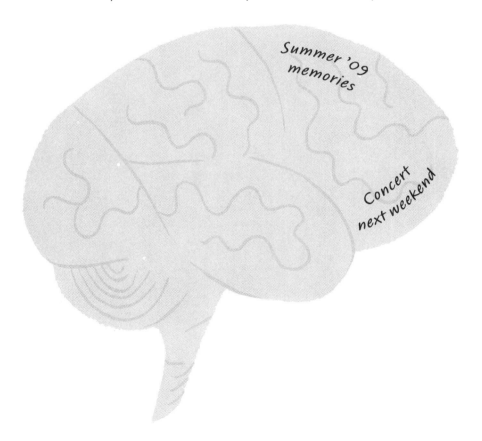

Summer '09 memories

Concert next weekend

Breathe In Hope

It can be hard to look forward to things when you're in a cycle of worry. Is there even anything to look forward to when everything feels so hopeless? Of course there is! All you need is a little reminder. In this activity, you're going to use the space on these two pages to "breathe in" hope by drawing every- thing you have to be excited for in the outline of lungs provided. Whether big or small, everything that makes you hopeful should be included. Not only will the mindful activity of drawing pull you out of your worries; it will also help reframe your fear of the unknown into the joy of possibility!

Put It on the Shelf

Sometimes a worry is worth thinking about at some point, but the current moment is not always the best time. Maybe you're about to go into a big presentation at work, or you're at a close friend's wedding, so it's best to put that worry away for a little while until there is a better opportunity. Of course, it can be difficult to set worry aside, which is where this activity comes in! Here, you're going to physically put (in other words, write or draw) your worry on this shelf to come back to later. It is your life: You get to decide what you do and when—worry does not!

Try 4-7-8 Breathing

Mindful breathing is a great way to calm worried thoughts and re-center yourself in the present moment. This simple breathing exercise can be done while sitting or lying down in a comfortable location.

instructions

1   First, place one hand on your belly and the other on your chest.

2   Take a deep and slow breath in through your nose, counting to 4 as you inhale.

3   Hold your breath, counting to 7 as you do so.

4   Once you reach 7, slowly start to breathe out through your mouth. As you exhale, count to 8, trying your best to get all the air out by the time you finish counting.

5   Repeat steps 2 through 4 five to ten times, or until you feel calm.

Get Out of Your Own Way

Sometimes the biggest obstacle in your life is, well, *you*. And that's okay! It's part of human nature to resist change, self-sabotage, get in your head, and overthink things. And unfortunately that's also where worry creeps in. But it doesn't mean you can't take back the reins and steer around these roadblocks.

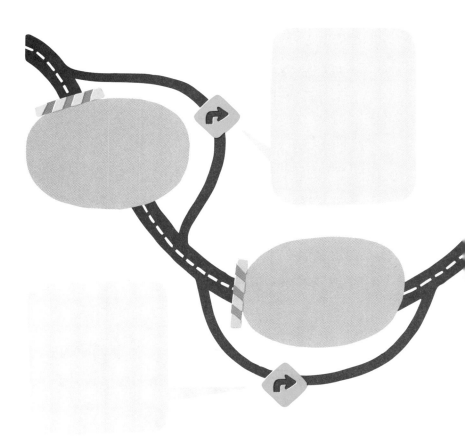

On this page and the previous one, you're going to write down different ways you make roadblocks for yourself. For example, you might get in your way by procrastinating. Then, next to each detour sign, you're going come up with a way to get around that roadblock, like breaking things down into tiny, bite-sized tasks to squash that urge to procrastinate.

Keep It—or Lose It!

It can be difficult to figure out which worries are worth exploring and which ones should be let go of. Fortunately, this handy checklist will help you do just that! Think about a current worry and go through the following checkboxes. If you check five or more, it's time to say a permanent goodbye to that worry.

- [ ] I have absolutely no control over the outcome.

- [ ] This worry is in the past.

- [ ] This worry is in the future.

- [ ] I did the best I could with the situation.

- [ ] This worry is stressing me out more than what is actually happening.

- [ ] This will not matter in ten years.

- [ ] If this were happening to a friend, I would tell them (honestly) not to worry about it.

- [ ] My mom said it would be fine.

- [ ] I've already made a plan for how I'm going to handle the situation if it happens.

- [ ] This worry feels more like an obsession than a worry.

Identify Your Inner Circle

Who you surround yourself with has a huge impact on how you feel—about life and about yourself. Great friends lift you higher, while bad friends leave you feeling depleted...and worried. So what does your social circle look like? Write the names of each of your closest friends in the left column. In the right column, write down *why* they're your friends. Things to consider: Are they kind? Supportive? When you're done, look over each friend and your notes about them to determine which friendships are worth continuing to invest in and which ones you may want to take a step back from.

MY PEOPLE	WHY

Thank Worry

Worry is often posed as the enemy, but often it is like that well-meaning but misguided friend who is just trying to help. Thanking a worry for its input is a great way to acknowledge that you're feeling worried—and it's okay—but that you're not letting it steer your life this time! In each thank-you note provided, thank a worry you have had recently for its input, but explain why you're going to go with your own gut feelings instead. For example: "Thank you for your input, but I choose to believe this problem will work itself out in its own time."

Thank you for your input, but... _____

_____

_____

_____

_____

_____

_____

Thank you for your input, but... _____

_____

_____

_____

_____

_____

_____

Thank you for your input,
but... _____

_____
_____

_____

_____

_____

_____

_____

Thank you for your input,
but... _____

_____

_____

_____

_____

_____

_____

_____

Thank you for your input,
but... _____

_____

_____

_____

_____

_____

_____

_____

Thank you for your input,
but... _____

_____

_____

_____

_____

_____

_____

_____

Take a Visual Vacation

Visualization is a great mindfulness exercise that can refocus your thoughts away from worry and back to the present moment. In this scenario, you're going to visualize the most peaceful place you can possibly think of. Of course, visualization can take some practice, so start by drawing out your chosen place in the space provided. Maybe it's the beach, or somewhere you used to love as a kid!

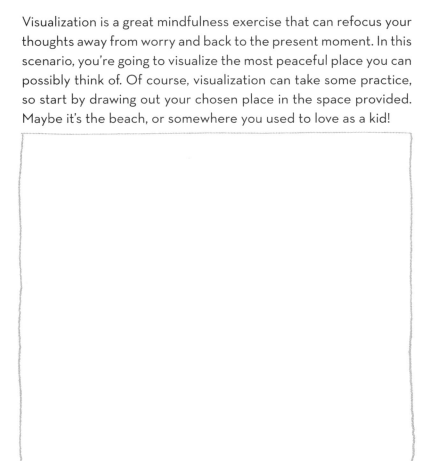

Once you draw out your destination, close your eyes and picture it in your mind. Try to tune in to the sensory details: What does it sound like? What's the temperature? These details will help you paint a more vivid picture and bring your mind to that place.

Set a Worry Timer

Sometimes you just need to worry it out. In this activity, you're going to set a timer on your smartphone for fifteen minutes to do just that. During these fifteen minutes, you're allowed to worry as much as you want. Once the timer goes off, it's time to step away from the worry and back into the present—no exceptions! Setting a worry timer gives you permission to honor what you feel without letting it completely take over, since you're only giving it fifteen minutes. You can use the rest of this page to plan out what you're going to do with the rest of your day, or to make a note of anything you learned or want to come back to in your next fifteen minutes.

Forget about Yourself!

It can be easy to worry about what someone else might be thinking of you. Maybe you think you've embarrassed yourself in some way, and now everyone *must* be obsessing over it just like you are. The truth is, though, that's just not the case! People aren't thinking about you nearly as much as you worry they are: Just like you, they're thinking about themselves. And that means one fewer thing for you to worry about.

In this activity, you're going to step into the shoes of the people around you. In each of the thought bubbles on these two pages, imagine what might be going on in the minds of people like your coworkers, neighbors, and even strangers you pass on the street. Think about the possible struggles they might be dealing with that are similar to yours—their busy workday, their family situations, etc. There is so much more than you on people's minds, and that's a good thing!

Tap Into Your Wise Mind

In Dialectical Behavior Therapy (DBT), there is a concept called "wise mind." It's the place where your rational mind and emotional mind meet. When you're in "wise mind," you're in the best possible mind-set to experience the world as it actually is. It helps you see the truth of a situation and think through problems in a comprehensive way. In this activity, you are going to tap into your wise mind to ease the worries that come from an imbalance of emotional and rational thinking. In the following Venn diagram, write out a current situation in the perspectives of your rational mind (the facts) and emotional mind (your emotions).

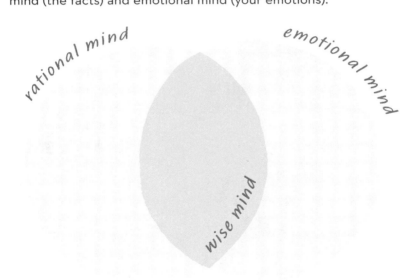

Now look at both viewpoints and what common ground they share. What compromises can you find? Write your observations in the "wise mind" space.

Put It Down

Your phone can be a huge source of worry. What's going on in the world of *Snapchat*? Who is unfollowing who on *Instagram*? Who posted a cryptic status on *Facebook*? It's time to put your phone down on this page and leave it there for at least one hour. Now look around you. What is going on in this moment? Take it all in.

PLACE PHONE HERE *for* *one hour*

Cash In These Free Freak-Out Passes

It's okay to freak out sometimes. In fact, it might even be necessary! Self-expression is a vital part of being human, after all, and releasing emotion can be just like hitting a reset button for your brain. Here you will find your free passes to freak out during those times when life gets to be too much. When you use a freak-out pass, write down exactly what's bothering you on that pass, then give yourself fifteen, thirty, or even sixty minutes to feel it all.

★ ONE FREE ★
FREAK-OUT

★ ONE FREE ★
FREAK-OUT

★ ONE FREE ★
FREAK-OUT

★ ONE FREE ★
FREAK-OUT

★ ONE FREE ★
FREAK-OUT

★ ONE FREE ★
FREAK-OUT

Unwind with Aromatherapy

Aromatherapy is the soothing practice of using natural oils to improve your psychological and physical state. These oils can be diffused through a handy oil diffuser, added to a diffuser necklace or bracelet, or applied directly to the skin (be sure to read warning labels and directions carefully). There are several essential oils that are known specifically to reduce worry. These are:

Use one or more of these oils in moments of distress and feel their relieving effects wash over you. You can find essential oils online or at your local health food store.

Make Your Own Light

Where there is darkness, there is always light. Sometimes it will present itself on its own, and sometimes you may need to create it yourself. It's important to remember that you always have the power to make your own light, even in the darkest of times. Draw a flame on the following candle. You can make it small and simple, or big and vibrant. You can color it any way you want, or use a pen or pencil: It's your flame to create!

See, you can always find the light!

Unleash Your Inner Warrior!

You are not a worrier; you are a warrior! Of course, this can be pretty hard to remember when you are caught up in a spiral of worry. Fortunately, this activity is here to remind you! In the chart provided here, list moments of past worry.

WORRIER

In the chart on this page, list the ways you have fought through those moments and prevailed. For example, maybe you were scared to give a speech, but you got up there and killed it. You are not just someone who worries; you are someone who triumphs!

WARRIOR

Relax with Guided Meditation 4:
LET THAT STUFF GO

Meditation is the practice of quieting worried or chaotic thoughts by refocusing your mind on the present moment. In this guided meditation, you are going to let go of all the things holding you back: the fears, the past—everything you can't control. You'll first record yourself reading the following steps, then you'll play the recording back to yourself to complete the meditation.

instructions

1 Find a position that is comfortable, in a quiet environment.

2 Take a deep breath in through your nose. Feel yourself sink into this moment.

3 Exhale through your mouth slowly. As you do, envision yourself breathing out everything you're worrying about.

4 Breathe in again through your nose. Allow all that you cannot control to exist as it is, without intervention, without resistance.

5 Breathe it out through your mouth. Let it go and feel yourself become free.

6 Continue breathing in and then out until you feel the worries melt away.

Follow Your Passion, Not Your Fear

In life, you have many opportunities to make a decision. In fact, it's estimated that you make thirty-five thousand decisions each *day*! Of those, you will probably come to at least one choice that is a fork in the road: Either you follow a fear or a passion. You don't have to go down that road of fear! Instead, you can go down the road of passion, following something that might make you happy. So it's time to take the reins! First, think about a choice you are faced with (or may be in the near future). On the left side of the fork, write down what you are afraid of when it comes to this choice (maybe there are risks involved, etc.). On the right side, write down the decision you would make if you were unafraid.

FEAR / PASSION

Now visualize yourself taking that second path—and do it!

Take the Scenic Route

Sometimes, it's easy to worry that you're falling behind everyone else. Whether it's seeing yet another engagement announcement (while you're single...still) or watching yet another friend receive a killer promotion while you're stuck in a job you're not even sure you *like*, it's hard to put things in perspective, and even harder to see what you *do* have going for you. Luckily that's what this activity is for! We have provided two paths. One represents your journey, while the other represents the journey of a friend, former classmate, or family member. In your path, you're going to write down all your accomplishments over the years, and in the other, you're going to write their accomplishments.

The truth is, comparisons aren't all bad: They can actually be a great tool for putting things into perspective and seeing that a different path doesn't equal a less successful one. Even though you might feel a little jealous and a little off track at times, you have things that others don't—things they might even be a little envious of themselves!

my

JOUR-NEY

their

JOUR-NEY

Fill 'Er Up!

Worry is so good at draining the energy right out of you in no time, which means you're less equipped to deal with it the next time it comes around, and even *less* the time after that, until eventually you're stuck in an exhaustive cycle. To avoid this pattern of worry, it's important to refuel your emotional tank regularly. So what fuels *you*? Your friends? Your job? Your hobbies? In the tank here, write down anything that gives you energy and leaves you feeling refreshed. Then do one of those things! Worry will always be part of life, but so will joy—you just need to make the space for it.

Defy Gravity

A relaxed state of mind can make you feel light as a feather. All your worries are lifted away, and you are left with that airy feeling of contentment. In this activity, you're going to encourage this light-as-a-feather feeling by planning for moments of regular relaxation. In the following feathers, write down the different activities that make you feel relaxed, from a warm bath to spending time with friends. Make sure each day includes one of these activities—even if just for a few minutes between that work assignment and a family obligation.

Play "Ten Questions" with Worry

It's time to get a little curious about your worry. After all, the more you understand something, the less scary it is! On the next page, you're going to play a round of "Ten Questions" with a worry. Go through the list and ask it each question as though it were a person you were talking to. You can also record the answers on a separate piece of paper. As you start looking at worry from a place of interest rather than fear, you can put that thought into more perspective and work through the hang-ups that have made it difficult to let go of. Let's play!

On this EPISODE of TEN QUESTIONS

1 What thought or feeling did you come from?

2 Has something similar happened before?

3 How did that turn out?

4 So, what's the worst that could happen?

5 How likely is that?

6 What are some things I can do to mitigate the bad?

7 What are some things I can do to increase the good?

8 How long has this been an issue?

9 How long will this likely be an issue?

10 How are you serving me?

Stop the Burnout

When you are burning the candle at both ends, worry starts to build. It thrives on the exhaustion and the lack of self-care that come with taking on more than you should—for longer than you should. In this activity, you're going to explore the ways you're burning yourself out and how this is causing more worry and stress than you may have realized. (For example, maybe you have been refusing to delegate tasks at work.)

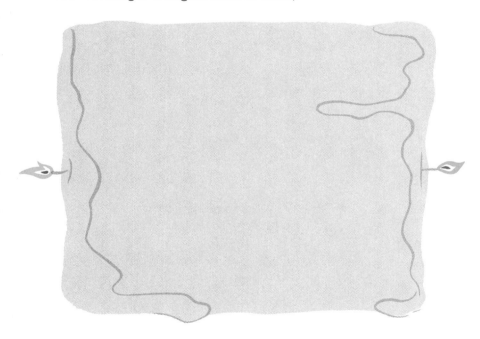

Now, highlight a few habits or tasks in the candle that you can get rid of now. When you finally give yourself permission to let go a little, you can begin to feel less worried.

Apply Your Mask!

In the event of a crisis on an airplane, the flight attendants always say that you need to put your own mask on before assisting others. After all, without a proper oxygen supply you can't help anyone else. The same goes for your everyday life. When you get caught up in worry, it is easy to neglect your well-being, putting it behind deadlines, friend problems, and everything else. But it is so important that you remember it is not selfish to put yourself first. In fact, it is necessary. Just like with oxygen masks on an airplane, you can't tend to the other people and things in life if you are mentally or physically exhausted. Whenever you have the urge to neglect your personal health, it is helpful to repeat a mantra that reminds you that you are worthy of care. Use the space provided to create some affirming mantras of your own. I've filled in a couple to get you started:

* Self-care is not selfish
* I come first
*
_____

_____

*
_____

_____

*
_____

_____

Update Your Status!

Think about what you see on your *Facebook* and *Instagram* newsfeeds: New babies. Weddings. Promotions. There aren't a whole lot of the less glamorous human parts, are there? And when you're constantly faced with the picture-perfect, it's easy to feel pressure to live up to that impossible standard.

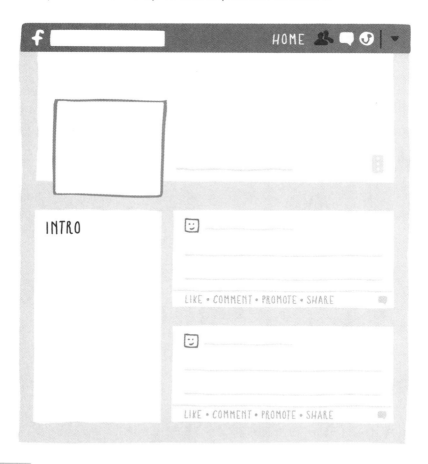

It's time to set the record straight—for yourself. Here, you're going to create a fake *Facebook* profile of everything you don't share on *Facebook*: spilling your coffee on your shirt, your messy kitchen, a fight with a friend. It's your chance to let go of being perfect and embrace being *real*!

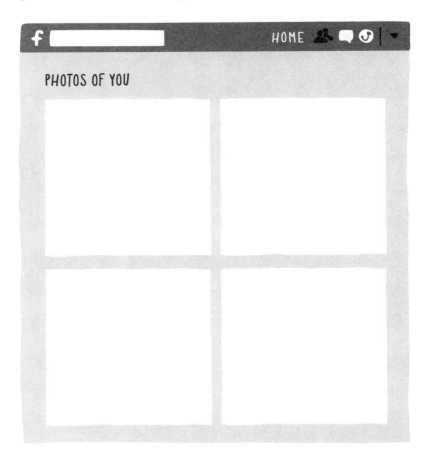

Color Your Way to Calm: Roller-Coaster

Life is a roller-coaster—
grab your colored
pencils and
enjoy the
ride!

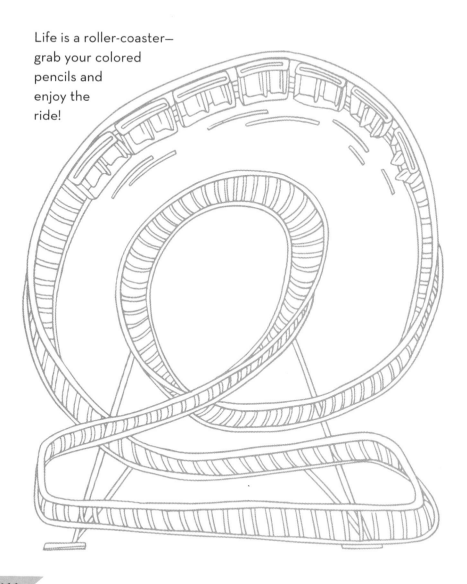

Swipe Left!

In a lot of ways, worry is like a bad partner: It brings you down, clings to you when you're desperate for alone time, and tries to convince you that you need it. So isn't it high time you looked at worry for what it really is? In the space provided, fill in a dating profile for worry—and make it honest. For example, you can write about how worry is a liar.

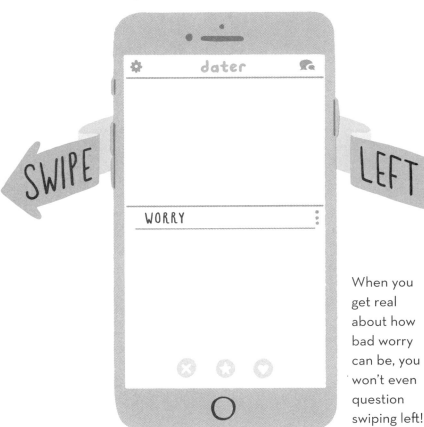

dater

WORRY

When you get real about how bad worry can be, you won't even question swiping left!

Keep an "Almost Missed It!" Log

When you get too deep inside your own head (thanks a *lot*, worry), it's impossible to see what's in front of you—so you end up missing a lot of really great things. Of course, you can't shut off worry for good (and sometimes it can be a useful tool you wouldn't *want* to get rid of), but you can move a little closer to less worry by making space in your life for appreciating the times when you aren't consumed by fearful thoughts. What things do you notice when you *are* living in the present moment? A joke between friends sitting near you? A puppy walking down the street? In the space on the next page, you're going to start a log of things you see, hear, smell, touch, or even taste when you're tuned in to the present—things you would have missed if you had been agonizing about the past or worrying about the future. Continue your log in a notebook or a notes app on your smartphone.

My LOG:

DATE	ALMOST MISSED...

Put It on Your Plate

Worry likes to creep in when you feel like there is so much to do that you can't even wrap your head around it all. In these cases, it can be helpful to get down everything you need to do. Seeing it on paper will allow you to sort through different tasks and toss out what isn't necessary so you can make more room for what is. So what's on your plate? Draw or write it down on the plate. As you complete tasks, you can also cross them out here for an extra sense of accomplishment.

Embrace the Butterflies

You know those butterflies you get in your stomach? Usually they're associated with scary situations that you can't wait to be out of (ahem, public speaking...). But they can also be a source of excitement! With a little shift in thinking, that fluttery feeling can be an opportunity for something great—like that time you were nervous about applying for graduate school but then got that acceptance letter. In this space, you're going to start that shift by filling in each butterfly with an experience that you were worried about but that ended up being an exciting or even crucial moment.

Track Your Body

How you take care of your physical health can play a big role in how well you're able to cope with worry. For example, ten cups of coffee will definitely send your thoughts into overdrive, while working out releases feel-good hormones that can nip worry in the bud.

DAY	CAFFEINE	SUGAR	EXERCISE
M			
T			
W			
T			
F			
S			
S			

In the charts provided, you're going to track caffeine, sugar, and water intake, as well as exercise, for one week. At the end of each day, rate your worry from 1 (minimal or no worry) to 10 (freaking out!!). Notice what might have changed between particular days. Did you consume a ton of sugar on a level 10 day?

DAY	WATER	OTHER	WORRY
M			
T			
W			
T			
F			
S			
S			

Take Back the Driver's Seat

You're in the driver's seat of your own life. While detours can be expected—and there'll absolutely be some bumps along the way—you're in control of how you act (and react). Unfortunately, worry is often trying to convince you otherwise. So it's time to reclaim the driver's seat and shut down those lies worry has been telling you. In this windshield, draw or write the "roadblocks" created by your worries lately. What awful things are they saying are up ahead? Then, either near these roadblocks or on a separate piece of paper, write how you would "steer" around these obstacles if they happened. How would you react in order to get back on track?

Find the Beauty in Being Imperfect

My BEAUTIFUL
IMPERFECTIONS

* _____
* _____
* _____
* _____
* _____
* _____
* _____
* _____

There is so much beauty in imperfection. For one thing, you'd be so, so boring if you always got everything right! If you never misstepped, belly-flopped, or dealt with a less-than-perfect emotion, you'd have a lot less to talk about and, more importantly, a lot less to learn from. Unfortunately, it can be hard to remember the good things about imperfection when you are right in the thick of a mistake or a trying situation—and that's where this activity comes in. In the space here, you're going to make a list of all your beautiful imperfections. Whenever the worry that you aren't good enough, capable enough, or just plain *enough* comes creeping in, reread your list!

ABOUT THE AUTHOR

MOLLY BURFORD is a writer, editor, and social media strategist. Her writing has appeared in *Allure, Teen Vogue,* and *Thought Catalog,* among others. Molly was born and raised in Detroit and now resides in Denver. She loves her family, friends, all dogs, and pasta. Learn more at MollyBurford.com.